WYATT TEE WALKER

SPIRITS THAT DWELL IN DEEP WOODS I

The Prayer and Praise Hymns
of the Black Religious Experience

Musical Notations and Arrangements

by

C. Eugene Cooper

with a foreword

by

GARDNER C. TAYLOR

MARTIN LUTHER KING FELLOWS PRESS®

SPIRITS THAT DWELL IN DEEP WOODS

Copyright 1987

Martin Luther King Fellows Press New York, N.Y. 10026

All rights reserved. No part of this publication may be reproduced, stored in a retrieval system, or transmitted in any form or by any means eletronic, mechanical, photocopying, recording or otherwise except for brief quotations included in review of book.

Library of Congress Cataloging in Publication Data

Walker, Wyatt Tee
  Spirits That Dwell in Deep Woods
  1. Afro-American Music,2. Music of the Black Church, 3. Afro-American Folklore, includes notes.

LC 87-060988
ISBN 0-937644-09-9

Cover design by Ray Leonardo
Copy editor Judith Price
Typeset in Trump 12 pt.

Printed and bound by Ray Leonardo & Sons, Valhalla, N.Y.

The name Martin Luther King Fellows Press is registered as a trademark in the U.S. patent office

Reprinted - 1992      Printed in the U.S.A

DEDICATION

*To all of the members
of the
SILVER STRANDS
past and present
from whose memory banks
this treasure was mined*

Other Publications by Wyatt Tee Walker

Books

THE BLACK CHURCH LOOKS AT THE BI-CENTENNIAL
SOMEBODY'S CALLING MY NAME
CHINA DIARY
THE SOUL OF BLACK WORSHIP
ROAD TO DAMASCUS
OVERCOMING STRESS, Contributor
COMMON THIEVES
SPIRITS THAT DWELL IN THE DEEP WOODS
ADAM, ROCKY AND MARTIN*

Essays

Nothing But A Man: The Historical Significance of Malcolm X
Liberation Theology and the Conflict in the Middle-East
The Role of the Black Church in the Revolution of the 60's
Leadership Needs For Tomorrow's Churches
A Tribute to the Mothers of South Africa*

*scheduled for release late fall 1987

ACKNOWLEDGEMENTS

The initial thanks for this work is appropriately extended to our foremothers and forefathers whose indomitability of spirit and tenacity of faith provided our sacred music tradition with this treasure. Undoubtedly, some were ex-slaves in their declining years and others were their children who endured another form of bondage in Jim Crow America. Somehow we must re-capture the spiritual genius they developed in the midst of psychic and spiritual want imposed on them only because of their burnished skins. There is no way that I know to establish the authorship of these hymns although each had its beginning in some single heart. The oral tradition kept them alive and the community of faith shaped them to their present form. In a way, perhaps that is best, for it has come to us as a collective legacy of faith for the dark days around us.

Secondly, I am indebted to that great spirit, Gardner C. Taylor, who inadvertently provided me with the arresting title for this work. Dr. Taylor was gracious enough to write the foreword for an earlier work in this field, *Somebody's Calling My Name*. He lifted up a quote from Booker T. Washington that seized my imagination so strongly that I vowed to write a book suited to that particular phrase. Washington was describing a "mini-Pentecost" when slaves gathered in the "quarters" and communally "...sang for hours in the evening around the fire of war, hunting, *spirits that dwell in deep woods....*" That phrase suggested to me the mystical spirituality of our people. This work seems to certify that spirituality and thus its title.

Then some continuing word of thanks to that scholar of African American religious practice, Henry H. Mitchell. Dr. Mitchell has just finished a season serving as Dean of the Graduate School of Religion of my alma mater, Virginia Union University at Richmond. It was Mitchell who plowed the early ground, conceptualizing in print, the religious connection between Africa and her descendants in this land. He created and implemented the Martin Luther King Program in Black Curriculum Studies at Colgate Rochester Divinity School. It was Mitchell who nominated this writer to that doctoral program which opened the door to the discipline of writing, research and publication. That program became permanent with the founding of the Martin Luther King Fellows Press under whose imprimatur this work appears.

I am grateful to the Canaan family at every level for its inspiration, support and encouragement. Especial thanks are due the Prayer Band and the Silver Strands. The congregation's musical director, my colleague and friend, C. Eugene Cooper, collaborated with me on the musical analysis and provided the arrangements included in the text and deserves special mention.

Samuel DeWitt Proctor, Abyssinian's (N.Y.) Senior Pastor, was good enough to read the early manuscript. Jeremiah Wright, Senior Minister of Trinity United Church of Christ in Chicago(a musicologist in his own right) read the final draft critically and his comments strenghthened this effort.

Finally, my wife, sweetheart and friend, Theresa Ann, has faithfully read the different drafts of this work as I have made revisions. The patience and love she provides eases the tedium of completing so bold a task as this. Judith Price Shirley was helpful in the final proof-reading of the galleys.

Wyatt Tee Walker
Marseille, France
16 August 1986

AUTHOR'S PREFACE

In the course of completing a doctoral study that focused on the music of the Black religious experience and its impact on social change, I became aware of an identifiable and distinct music-form that was not included in my work. The scheme for my dissertation on Black sacred music on the North American continent embraced *Spirituals, Black Meter Music, Hymns of Improvisation, Historic and Modern Gospel.* * Sixty thousand words into my study, I realized there was this body of musical literature *still in use*, that traced its origins to the prayer meetings and pre-service devotionals of Black religious life. I arbitrarily named this music, the *Prayer and Praise Hymns of the Black Religious Experience*.

Many of these hymns are used today in the identical settings in which they were born. At that particular moment in time(1974), this genre of music did not fit into the typology tht I had developed for my study. I concluded with some tinge of guilt, that I was too far along to re-structure my work.

For the last ten years, I have methodically collected and researched this family of religious folk-music. My primary source has been the memory banks of countless individuals, lay and clergy, who with gentle prodding, called to memory these gems of faith from days long since past. This is the music that I have named the *Prayer and Praise Hymns*. I settled on this label because of the arena in which they have been coined and nurtured to survival - the prayer meetings and pre-service devotionals of Black Church life.

* See *Somebody's Calling My Name*, Judson Press: Valley Forge, Pa., 1979.

FOREWORD

The probing mind of Dr. Wyatt T. Walker has given us an engaging sequel to his classic study, "Somebody's Calling My Name", in "Spirits That Dwell in Deep Woods." The title itself is haunting and mysterious, being a phrase used in the long ago by Booker Washington to describe evenings in his slave childhood when families sat around the fire and talked about the puzzling moods and cryptic insights which came to them with a vividness so strong that they seemed to be an embodiment, a personal presence.

It may be that all worthy music is born of such mystery, so immediate that it requires response in rhyme and tune - since ordinary language becomes hopelessly frail under such circumstance. Dr. Walker has examined that Christian music of black people which was born out of the puzzling circumstance following an emancipation whose promise was never quite met, leaving the freedmen no longer slaves, but not free, either. In that paradox the music examined here came into being. We are all indebted to Dr. Walker for lifting up this music of a people's passing from American slavery and through a wilderness, long and dreary, beyond which so many have dared believe there lies the Promised Land of full citizenship both in the country of their birth and in that better country where believers are "going home to live with Jesus."

Gardner C. Taylor
Brooklyn, N.Y.

TABLE OF CONTENTS

	Page
Acknowledgments	v
Author's Preface	vii
Foreword	ix
Introduction	1

Chapter One
  BLESSED BE THE NAME OF THE LORD 5

Chapter Two
  GREAT CHANGE SINCE I BEEN BORN 13

Chapter Three
  GLORY, GLORY! HALLELUJAH 23

Chapter Four
  I KNOW I GOT RELIGION, YES, YES 33

Chapter Five
  LORD HAVE MERCY 41

Chapter Six
  I'M GLAD I GOT THAT OLD TIME RELIGION 49

Chapter Seven
  I KNOW MY NAME IS WRITTEN THERE 59

Chapter Eight
  TALKIN' 'BOUT A GOOD TIME 69

Postscript 79

Notes 81

INTRODUCTION

The Prayer and Praise Hymns have been an integral part of the sacred hymnody of the Black religious experience. Following the disappointment of the Post-reconstruction era, Black religious practice turned increasingly inward. Though the children of slaves borrowed from and adapted some of the worship styles of the dominant society (whites), the practical reality of the separateness in American life induced in African Americans, a form of self-reliance so far as the character of our worship styles were concerned. Black people trudged ahead with their Africanized version of Christianity, coping as best we could with the persistent presence of racism and color prejudice.

Emigration from the rural South was not widespread. At the turn of the century, large numbers of Blackamericans remained in the countryside working the land they owned or sharecropping. It was in the rural South, principally, that these hymns were born.

These hymns are not *Spirituals* in either the technical or historical sense. All authentic *Spirituals* antedated the end of the Civil War. Neither are they *Black Meter Music* in any sense, though much of the verbiage is drawn from the bright imagery of the latter part of the meter music era. They are adaptations of what rural Blacks heard around them religiously. The poetry and musicality of the *Prayer and Praise Songs* are distinct from that of spirituals and Black meter music.

In time frame, these songs are spin-offs of the early hymn-book era in Black religious life (c. 1885-1925).[1] They are in every sense, folk-music of the Black religious experience. Like the spirituals, in this respect, there are no identifiable authors. The body of this music expresses in individual form the collective consciousness of the community in matters of religious belief. There is in this music the flavor of both *Spiritual and Black Meter Music* without any real loss of its own identity.

The primary purpose of this introductory word is to provide a general profile of this music-form to avoid unneccessary repetition in the body of the general text. The several parts of this profile are applicable to nearly all of the hymns of this music family.

There are no hymns which are not *Bible-Based*. It is not difficult to fix the explicit and implicit reference in the Scriptures. This is no surprise given the influence of the spirituals in the musicality of the Black community generally and in religious life particularly. The practice of religion among Blacks on the North American continent reveals clearly that we are essentially people of the Book. Our religious faith and practice centers in the authority of the Bible.

All of these songs are of *southern origin*. At the beginning of the twentieth century, no mass migrations to the industrial centers of the North had yet taken place. The predominant population of African Americans remained in the South and the border states. There had been as noted earlier, measurable shifts of population to the urban centers of the South but not in sufficient numbers to deplete the rural of a sizable Black community.

The character of this music betrays its rural roots. The repetition, which we shall turn to in a moment, reveals that the *oral tradition* was still operative.[2] Its presence was as much out of need as it was cultural for Blacks in the rural South. In spite of Freedom schools and literacy training, many, many New World Africans were barely literate. The hymnbook was coming into broad use after the turn of the century, but literacy rates were abysmally low in the rural. These hymns of faith are by no means the product of an urban environment. Their formation was distinct and separate from piano and/or organ accompaniment.

The *repetitive character* to which we have already alluded served primarily as a memory device for these rural residents of the South who had very narrow access to literacy training. Again, the meager resources in the rural South made the likelihood of hymnbooks rare and the purchase of pianos and organs even more rare. This repetitive quality is a direct descendant of the *Spiritual's* influence whose antecedent was the repetitive music of West Africa. All are tied together in the tradition of oral transmission with repetition being one of its primary devices.

The *restricted literary form* was directly influenced by the repetitive character. Rhyme was only of secondary importance. The most frequently occurring poetic forms are the *a a a b* and the *a a b a*. Next in frequency is the *ab ab ab ab* and the *double a a a b*. Occasionally, there is also *a a b c a* and *a b a c* with variations of the others noted above.

Nearly half of these praise hymns extant make broad use of the *traveling couplet* and the *quatrain form* for stanza material. The traveling couplet form was born with the spirituals and used in precisely the same random manner. The quatrain form was introduced to frontier America by Dr. Isaac Watts and the Wesley brothers, John and Charles. African Americans "borrowed" what was useful and attractive to their spiritual appetites.

The musical modality of these songs is similar. Most of the melodies can be charted on the *pentatonic scale* (five notes). With rare exception, the music is *rhythmic* though there are a few numbers that are measured and slow moving. The imagery is in the folk-idiom drawn from the everyday experiences of the plain and simple people of the land who gave birth to this family of music. All are *testimonial* in character and deeply personalized as evidence of God's encounter with their lives.

In the body of this work, each hymn selected is analyzed individually. Each has its own message and witness in song. The chapter begins with the musical notation in four part harmony facing the full lyrics (so far as possible) on the page opposite. The narrative accompanying the hymn opens with a brief word of introduction to that specific hymn.

There follows the general exposition that includes the *Biblical Basis*, the *Theological Mooring, Lyric and Form Analysis and Contemporary Significance*. It is my hope that this seminal work will underscore the need to preserve in permanent form this treasure of faith.

BLESSED BE THE NAME OF THE LORD

BLESSED BE THE NAME OF THE LORD

BLESSED BE THE NAME OF THE LORD

BLESSED BE THE NAME OF THE LORD

In all my appointed time
I'm gonna wait 'till my change comes
In all my appointed time
I'm gonna wait 'till my change comes
In all my appointed time
I'm gonna wait 'till my change comes
(Job said) The Lord giveth
(Job said) The Lord taketh
(Job said) Blessed be the name of the Lord

Servant he come runnin'
(Sayin') All your sheeps is gone
Servant he come runnin'
(Sayin') All your sheeps is gone
Servant he come runnin'
(Sayin') All your sheeps is gone
(Job said) The Lord giveth
(Job said) The Lord taketh
Blessed be the name of the Lord

Servant he come runnin' (3x)
(Sayin') All your camels gone
(Job said) The Lord giveth
(Job said) The Lord taketh
Blessed be the name of the Lord

Servant he come runnin' (3x)
(Sayin') All yo' children dead
(Job said) The Lord giveth
(Job said) The Lord taketh
Blessed be the name of the Lord

1

BLESSED BE THE NAME OF THE LORD

The Story of Job

Introduction

    This prayer-hymn is unique in that it embraces the narrative of the Job story in song.[1] It provides an unusual literary form that has to be considered advanced for the period of its origin. The literary form and musicality of this song combine to produce a music piece of rare beauty. What is most compelling, is that the simple and plain people of the rural South possessed such fundamental musical genius to incorporate into song one of the most perplexing theological issues of religious faith: *Why do the righteous suffer?*

    This narrative prayer-hymn begins and ends with Job's much-heralded conclusion of faith: "...all the days of my appointed time will I wait, till my change comes."[2] "Blessed be the name of the Lord...." is only added affirmation of trust and faith in God. When mirrored against the social circumstance in which this hymn was fashioned (early twentieth century rural America), this was an effective morale boost for hard-pressed Blackamericans who believed in the ultimate goodness and justice of God.

Biblical Basis

    No one could miss the answer to the question as to the Biblical basis of this prayer-hymn. So transparent is the explicit Biblical reference, it seems almost redundant to explore any discussion in this regard. As noted earlier, this song is a summary digest of the Job story and is a distinct "type". Few others, if any, tell a complete Bible story. Most include passing references to Bible incidents but few focus narrowly on a single narrative as does *Blessed Be the Name of the Lord.*

It is quite remarkable that the hymn-poem includes nearly every event of the Job saga with a clear statement of faith concerning the vicissitudes of life. So complete is the essential story of Job, one almost wishes there was some mention of Eliphaz the Temanite, Bildad the Shuite and Zophar the Naamathite.[3]

Theological Mooring

The survival of this prayer-hymn via the oral tradition of the Black religious experience, is testimony to the tightly held Christian view of perseverance and the ultimate sovereignty of God. Given the social context of the people who authored this musical piece, one understands more clearly why this hymn still lives. The hope of any oppressed people that has no theological grounding in accepting what God gives without altogether understanding, will soon collapse and die. The Job syndrome is part and parcel of the Afro-American religious experience in the United States. It has never been easy for Black people to survive in white America. Our tenacity and unwarranted hope in the face of old brutalities (slavery) and new brutalities (Graham-Rudmann) is rooted in the heroic declaration of Job: "Though He slay me, yet will I trust Him."[4] This prayer-hymn lives largely because the social context of Black Americans has changed so little. We see in "Job's children", the indomitability of spirit so necessary to creative faith and practice.

The refrain affirms at the outset the "case" that it is making: whatever our lot in life, God allows it and however good or ungood our fortunes, God's name be praised! The stanzas follow the Job sequence of the Scriptures. In some southern communities, another stanza, similar to the first two, is used:

> *Servant he come runnin'*
> *(Saving)All your oxen gone...etc,"*

We can never be absolutely sure how much of the original

song remains extant. In any event, this unique prayer-hymn is a genuine treasure of the Black sacred music tradition.

Lyric and Form Analysis

In all my appointed time	a
I'm gonna wait 'till my change comes	b
In all my appointed time	a
I'm gonna wait 'till my change comes	b
In all my appointed time	a
I'm gonna wait 'till my change comes	b
(Job said)The Lord Giveth	c
(Job said)The Lord Taketh	d
Blessed be the name of the Lord	e

The form analysis above illustrates clearly that *Blessed Be the Name of the Lord* is virtually one of a kind. In the more than one hundred hymns that I have charted, none that I have matches this hymn of faith in the literary sense. It does possess the fundamental earmarks of the *Prayer and Praise Songs:* it is repetitive in both the lyric and melodic line and its musicality is easily adaptable to group participation. Further, it contains some semblance of the "call and response" device, somewhat common to this music. "Job said" and "saying" are really more like interjections to maintain the musical and metric balance but also are responded to by the phrase immediately following. The literary form in the refrain is a variation of other forms that remain extant (shown at beginning of this section). The same formula is used throughout the stanzas.

As to the musical piece, it has its own distinct melody, a great many hymns of this body of music which have identical literary form also share nearly identical hymn-tunes. *Blessed Be the Name of the Lord* is unique in this regard. It is separate and distinct unto itself. The musicality of this hymn as well as the message, has contributed largely to its staying power within the family of free Black churches in the United States.

Contemporary Significance

The universality of trouble and suffering in human life

makes this hymn as useful as the Book of Job. Since it is a direct excerpt, it has the double advantage of fulfilling a specific need and serving as an introduction and/or primer on the Bible story itself. The fact that the basic message is set to music is of no little import. I do not believe it is possible to be an earnest Christian without acknowledgement of the Job-syndrome in life. Trial and suffering always seems to be without rhyme or reason.

As modern as we are, we have inherited some ancient ideas that plague us in the face of adversity. In Jesus' day, his disciples were confused on the issue of the relationship of sin to suffering.[5] The Bible is clear: all sin leads to suffering of some sort but conversely, not all suffering is due to sin. This understanding of this distinction is sorely needed in contemporary religious practice. Too often, a calamity or tragedy starts individuals on a guilt-trip endeavoring to pin-point the precise mis-deed(sin) that precipitated an unhappy circumstance. We are reminded in this folk-hymn that there are some things God *allows.* "...the rain *falleth on the just and unjust....*" Job and this Prayer and Praise Hymn remind us that in whatever change life may bring, the stance of the true believer is *Blessed Be the Name of the Lord!*

GREAT CHANGE SINCE I BEEN BORN

GREAT CHANGE SINCE I BEEN BORN

GREAT CHANGE SINCE I BEEN BORN

Great change since I been born
Great change since I been born
Great change since I been born
Been a great change since I been born

Places I use' to go
I don't go no more
Places I use' to go
I don't go no more
Places I use' to go
I don't go no more
Been a great change since I been born

Things I use' to do
I don't do no more
Things I use' to do
I don't do no more
Things I use' to do
I don't do no more
Been a great change since I been born

Company I use' to keep
I don't keep no more
Company I use' to keep
I don't keep no more
Company I use' to keep
I don't keep no more
Been a great change since I been born

2

GREAT CHANGE SINCE I BEEN BORN

A Saint's Testimony

Introduction

So far as I have been able to determine this hymn comes right out of South Carolina's low country, the region south of Columbia. It has the distinct earmarks of the testimonial character of the *Prayer and Praise Hymns*. This song came to my attention through one of the original members of the Silver Strands, Sister Alice McNeal, a native of South Carolina. The central message is as the lyric describes, a "great change" has been effected in the life of the worshiper since turning to Jesus Christ.

It may be instructive here, to note that this family of music, as nearly all music of the Black religious experience, has a pronounced Jesus-emphasis. The verbiage of the prayers, preaching and song is heavily laced with Jesus references. If the references is not explicit, the strong inference is easily deciphered. This is understandable in light of the development of the practice of religion among New World Africans. The transcendentalism of West African traditional religious in combination with the immanence of Christianity produced the "Jesus-faith" of the antebellum era.[1] The musical literature of this tradition has naturally been influenced in the same wise. The "born" reference is the second birth concept that has its origin in the teaching of Jesus and so crucial in the practice of folk-religion of Americans of African descent.

Biblical Basis

The "born again" tradition of the Black religious experience is authentically Biblical. The tradition is not exclusive to the Black folk church but is certainly more pronounced than some others. Paul's second letter to the Corinthian Church contains the specific text and context out of which this hymn originated: "Therefore if any man(person) be in Christ, he is a new creature: old things are passed away; behold all things are become new".[2]

The idea of the second birth is at the center of New Testament faith. The antebellum slave community, early on, placed heavy emphasis on the "born again" experience as the first step to salvation. It seems only logical, then, that in the *Prayer and Praise Hymns* as in the *Spirituals*, there is frequent lyric reference to the "born again" experience. "Great Change" is crystal clear in its testimony about the "before" and "after" conduct of the individual whose life is anchored in the Lord Jesus Christ.

Theological Mooring

Jesus' famous late night conversation with Nicodemus is the basis of the Pauline teaching on the "new ceature" concept.[3] Paul has amplified his exposition on the "new birth" in light of its connection to and dependence on the Risen Christ.[4] In recent years, the phenomenon of "born again Christians" has come into vogue but it has always been the basic ingredient of any salvation-beginning among Black Christians of the free churches. It has always been in vogue with us.

It is quite remarkable that the slave devotees of Jesus Christ were able to isolate this fundamental truth and appropriate it as an integral part of their religious tradition in spite of the formal religious instruction of the masters who administered an overdose of "Thou shalt not steal" and "slaves obey your masters".[5] The "born again" idea continues to be a linch-pin of faith in the practice of Christianity among Afro-Americans. Its continuity has never been broken.

The importance of the message of this hymn is that it

makes a clear statement, as do the Scriptures, that commitment to Jesus Christ lays serious demands of ethics and conduct upon all who claim Lordship in Him. You cannot follow Jesus without a marked and *remarkable* change in behavior. In our human circumstance, much of our conduct is contextual; we behave according to where we are and what kind of company we are in. That's the significance of the stanzas that say "Places I used to go...etc. and "Company I use' to keep...etc." The environs in which one moves as well as the social circle are strong determinants of conduct and ethics. A change in social environment for the Christian has a salutary impact on behavior, thus the lyric "Things I use' to do, I don't do no more...." The refrain emphasizes the turning point of this "Great change...." It is grounded in the "born again" event-"since I been born".

Lyric and Form Analysis

Great change since I been born	a
Great change since I been born	a
Great change since I been born	a
Been a great change since I been born	b

This hymn possesses two literary forms that are slightly different. The refrain is classic *a a a b* with a slightly extended closing line. The stanzas, however, are an *ab ab ab c* with the identical, slightly extended, closing line.

Places I use' to go	a
I don't go no more	b
Places I use' to go	a
I don't go no more	b
Places I use' to go	a
I don't go no more	b
Been a great change since I been born	c

The difference in the literary form of refrain to verse is not peculiar to this hymn alone. There are several in the collection of my study which replicates this general form though the stanzas may be similar to the refrain or less similar. "I Know I Got Religion" is a later example of close similarity. In most instances, in spite of the similarity, small or great, the closing line of refrain and stanza are frequently identical in the lyric line as well as the melodic line. That is the case in this hymn under scrutiny.

The melody of this hymn though simple, is distinct. As noted in another place, the hymns that are *a a a b* in form, frequently share the identical melody. "Great Change" so far as I have been able to discern, has its own melody. The stanzas of this *Praise Hymn* are similar in syllable count to other stanzas found in altogether different melodies. It is usually the refrain of these hymns which stamp their identity rather than the stanzas and the verse.

One other characteristic of this song that appears in others from time to time is what I term an "unspoken" word or phrase. In performance, the sense of what is being sung is really what appears below as an example:

>(Been a)Great change since I been born
>(Been a)Great change since I been born
>(Been a)Great change since I been born
>(There's)Been a great change since I been born

Sometimes, a contrasting voice will interject the words in parentheses while the primary lyrics are sung by the group assembled. The language of these hymns is seldom exact and in this song, I have heard *was* substituted for *been*. The message remains the same regardless of which word is used.

"Great Change" exhibits the testimonial character of the *Prayer and Praise Hymns* on a matter of faith that speaks to every believer's experience.

Contemporary Significance

These hymns, as do the *Spirituals*, possess messages of faith that have lasting currency. No Christian will refute the basic message of this hymn. A "born again" Christian is a new person in Christ. Practically, we believe more than we live; there is often wide disparity between the ethical and moral demands of our Christian faith and our personal and private conduct. This hymn is a stern and clear reminder that Christians must "practice what they preach". The present great laxity in morals in our nation provides earnest Christians with broad opportunity to demonstrate in our lives that those who really are "in Christ" are different; we are indeed "in the world" but not "of the world". The theological doctrine of regeneration is the measuring stick to determine the spiritual growth in our lives "since I was born". "Great Change" induces in us the promptings to take inventory on our lives.

# GLORY, GLORY! HALLELUJAH!

GLORY, GLORY! HALLELUJAH!

(See additional verses)

GLORY, GLORY! HALLELUJAH!

Glory, Glory! Hallelujah!
Since I laid my burden down.
Glory, Glory! Hallelujah!
Since I laid my burden down.

I feel better, so much better,
Since I laid my burden down.
I feel better, so much better,
Since I laid my burden down.

Friends don't treat me like they use' to,
Since I laid my burden down.
Friends don't treat me like they use' to,
Since I laid my burden down.

Burden down, Lord, burden down,
Since I laid my burden down.
Burden down, Lord, burden down,
Since I laid my burden down.

I'm goin' home to live with Jesus,
Since I laid my burden down.
I'm goin' home to live with Jesus,
Since I laid my burden down.

3

GLORY, GLORY! HALLELUJAH!

A Song of Praise

Introduction

This *Prayer and Praise Hymn* reflects the puritan theology of the late nineteenth century. It is jubilant in its declaration that the victory over sin and Satan has been won. There is something of the spirit and symbolism of John Bunyan's *Pilgrim's Progress*. The decision to follow Christ is the "burden" laid down. The suggestion of the struggle with Satan is the exultation with which the testimony is made. *Glory, Glory! Hallelujah!* is a phrase loaded with relief and release, joy and thanksgiving. It is one of the most exclamatory verses to be found in this musical literature.

The contextual use is in revival meetings when "sinners" are saved and at Communion and covenant services when the saints recall with some nostalgia how they "first met the Lord". The use noted above is the most frequent though it is not the exclusive use. I have often heard this number used as a benedictory or "going home" hymn.

Glory, Glory! Hallelujah! is one of the simpler forms of this family of music. The *a b a b* poetic form is a little rare. In this prayer hymn, the melodic line is dominant in its identity.

Biblical Basis

There may be some mild difference of opinion as to precisely what "burden" refers. It is a safe assumption, given the nature and fabric of the folk-religion of Blacks of this era, that it has to do with the conversion experience. It *could* be a reference to some personal weakness, but that is probably too particular, given the widespread use of this hymn. If the latter view is held, a more specific reference would have been made. Folk-religion, folk-music, folk-ways are seldom subtle. We can safely presume that this reference is to conversion to Jesus Christ.

The "born again" experience in Black religious life is a dominant theme in the music appropriated to Black religious use. As noted earlier, the New Testament view is that it is the initial step of discipleship. Both Jesus and Paul are dogmatic in this respect. Thus, there's little difficulty in fixing the Biblical basis of this prayer hymn. The invitation of Jesus fits rather neatly: "Come unto me, all ye that labor and are heavy laden. Take my yoke upon you and learn of me, for my yoke is easy and my burden is light."[1]

The imagery of the release from "burden" is unmistakeable. Within the context of conversion, the responsibility of the Christian discipline versus the burden and guilt of sin, the invitation of Jesus would be welcomed by a person searching for wholeness.

There is no small significance to the declaration, "I feel better so much better, etc." That stanza alone argues strongly for the conversion idea. In the past and in the present, new converts always testify of the peace of mind and tranquility of spirit that accompanies accepting the Lord Jesus Christ as Saviour and Lord. Following the conversion theme, the testimony of this song underscores the "separateness" of Christians from the world- "Friends don't treat me like they use' to...." This phrase echoes the earlier Spiritual, "I told Jesus it would be all right if He changed my name"(a reference to conversion). A stanza following declares, "Jesus told me the world's gonna' hate you if I change your name," that establishes that separateness mentioned earlier. This hymn, if its testimony is about conversion, has its roots squarely in the New Testament "born again" experience.

Theological Mooring

It never ceases to amaze me that the poor and humble people of the land managed to wrestle successfully with the profound truths of Scripture. As did their antebellum ancestors, they digested piecemeal, information on Christianity from the dominant society and developed a religious faith that is Biblically sound. Consider, if you will, that most of the members of the community of faith that created this musical literature, were far from literate. The ground on which they stood was narrow in opportunity (by Western criteria) for enlightenment.

It is obvious from casual reflection on this hymn that the believer's perception is clear that the most important thing that occurs in a person's life is turning to Christ. That is the rationale for the glorious exultation. Within the Christian context, nothing is more important than the initial decision to follow Jesus. It is the ground root of salvation. "And we know that our old being has been put to death with Christ on his cross, in order that the power of the sinful self might be destroyed, so that the soul no longer be the slaves of sin."[2]

No Christian's faith can long survive in discontentment. The testimony that "I feel better, so much better, etc." exhibits satisfaction and contentment in the decision made. The progression in the stanzas manifests the willingness to pay the price of discipleship. "Friends don't treat me...." As the Apostle Paul makes clear, the followers of Christ are *in* the world but are not *of* the world.[3] The observable difference between Christians and non-Christians creates a tension that cannot be resolved.

Nineteenth century Protestant theology and hymnody always rounded out its thought with the assurance of eternal life. That nineteenth century influence mentioned earlier does not go wanting in this hymn. "Goin' home to live with Jesus" is a legitimate and reasonable premise of Christian expectation despite the frequent unwarranted criticism of being "otherworldly". All religions, Christianity included, possess an otherworldly character or they would not be a "religion". This last stanza certifies the theological mooring of this *Prayer and Praise Hymn.*

Lyric and Form Analysis

Glory, glory! Hallelujah.	a
Since I laid my burden down.	b
Glory, glory! Hallelujah.	a
Since I laid my burden down.	b

Glory, Glory! Hallelujah! is a rarity in this class of music due to its abbreviated poetic form. At this writing, I cannot recall another hymn that is *a b a b* in structure. There are several *a b a b a b a b* prayer hymns but not many in the short form. Quite naturally, the abbreviated lyric form requires an abbreviated melodic form. The lesson to be gleaned here is to appreciate the variety of forms and lack of rigidity in the creation of this music.

The poetry of the lyrics is straightforward and uncomplicated. The message of the refrain is as succinct as it is jubilant. The stanzas, though presented in traditional sequence might be sung in any sequence with the exception of the last stanza. Changing the order of the other stanzas will do no great violence to its essential message.

The melody of this hymn is "jubilee" in character. The melodic line of the two couplets have only slight differences in the repeating *a* and *b* lyric lines as revealed in the musical notation at the beginning of this chapter.

Contemporary Significance

The folk-character of this song and its brief simplicity make it an attractive music-piece for the uninitiated. There are a great many Christians and a sizable number of Black

Christians who are unaware of this body of music as an identifiable "group". Almost every one knows two or three spirituals but few contemporary Christians have a full appreciation of the theological underpinning of this family of Black sacred music. An introduction to this music might properly begin with this hymn because of the universal appeal of its central message. Every professing Christian can identify with his or her personal experience of conversion to Jesus Christ. The lively pace and simplicity of the melodic texture commends itself to easy appropriation for use in worship, formal or informal.

The family of faith in this present age needs to be reminded of the joy that flooded our lives when Jesus came into our hearts. It is a memory that deserves and requires continual reinforcement.

I KNOW I GOT RELIGION, YES, YES!

I KNOW I GOT RELIGION, YES, YES!

(See additional verses)

I KNOW I GOT RELIGION, YES, YES!

I know I got religion,(Yes, Yes!)
I know I got religion,(Yes, Yes!)
I know I got religion,(Yes, Yes!)
And the world can't do me no harm.

I know I've been converted;
Of this I'm not ashamed,
My soul is anchored in ma' Jesus
And the world can't do me no harm.

They put Paul and Silas in prison,
They locked them to the wall;
But the power came down from heaven
And razed those jailhouse walls.

Christ told his disciples:
"Now when I'm risen and gone;
The world will talk about you
But you must bear your 'bukes and scorn."

Some say give me silver,
Some say give me gold;
But I say give me Jesus,
Because He's precious to my soul!

I KNOW I GOT RELIGION

A Testimony of Faith

Introduction

This hymn is a classic example of the testimonial character of much of this body of music. I learned this hymn in the days of the "Movement" symbolized by Martin Luther King Jr. In the heat of the Atlanta Sit-in campaign, Otis Moss, then a seminary student, sang this hymn before addressing a mass meeting at the Wheat Street Baptist Church.[1] Upon inquiry, he responded that he had learned it from his grandmother who had raised him. Obviously its roots are deep in rural Georgia but its message is universal. It bespeaks the certitude of a soul who is grounded in the conviction of absolute faith in the Lord Jesus Christ. As indicated earlier, rhyme does appear but this hymn illustrates that it is secondary to meter (syllables) in the musical sense. The stanzas are somewhat balanced in the metrical sense but uneven so far as rhyme is concerned. All in all, it matches very closely the profile suggested in the Introduction to this work.

Biblical Basis

The Psalmist's admonition, "Let the redeemed of the Lord say so...." might well be the Scriptural prompting for this testimony of faith.[2] There comes immediately to mind again the midnight meeting of Jesus and Nicodemus and the eternal verity that "...you must be born again...."[3] The second stanza refers directly to the episode in Acts when

Paul and Silas were miraculously freed from a Phillipian jail.⁴ The third stanza has obvious reference to Jesus' warning to his early followers on the cost of discipleship. The last stanza, as it appears here, is a frequently recurring theme of the absolute Lordship of Christ. There is the reminder of Jesus' *Sermon on the Mount* in which our Lord instructs his disciples, "Lay not up for yourselves treasures upon earth, where moth and rust doth corrupt, and where thieves break through and steal: But lay up for yourselves treasures in heaven...."⁵

Theological Mooring

The refrain of this hymn emphasizes through repetition the firm resolve of the believer's faith and practice. A "born again" Christian is insulated from the temptations and trials of this life-"and the world can't do me no harm". The theological sense is not immunity from the changes that life brings but the capacity to get through those changes. That resolve of the witness provides much of the tenacity needed for life's journey.

The first quatrain, appropriately establishes the basis of this strong confidence- a crystal-clear sense of rebirth in Jesus Christ for which there is no apology or reservation. The verbiage is precise: "My *soul* is anchored...." It is not the life or the body of the witness, but the soul- that which is everlasting and eternal.

The second quatrain demonstrates the awareness of God's supra-physical powers in the lives of the faithful. Every now and then, God breaks in on the affairs of his people to reassure us that He cares about us in our impossible circumstances. Our hi-tech era has dismissed cavalierly the reality of the miraculous. The stanza following reflects the connection between the disciples of the Apostolic era and our discipleship today. True discipleship requires perserverance in the face of difficult times. The convenience and modernity of our times sometimes dulls our sensitivity to this aspect of discipleship.

The last stanza is an iteration of the choice of the Lord (spiritual values) over the world (temporal concerns). Mention has already been made of Jesus' admonition, "Lay not up for yourselves treasures on earth...." In another work, this writer has made a strong case that Black sacred music mirrors our sociology.[6] Another version of this last quatrain substitutes *freedom* for *Jesus*. It is usually sung as a reprise to the original form. Either form is altogether appropriate when one considers the predicament of the Afro-Americans today.

Lyric and Form Analysis

I know I got religion(Yes, Yes!)	a
I know I got religion(Yes, Yes!)	a
I know I got religion(Yes, Yes!)	a
And the world can't do me no harm	b

The refrain of this prayer hymn is cast in the *a a a b* form mentioned in the Introduction. The three identical lines with a closing second line appears more frequently in the *Prayer and Praise Songs* than any other. The hymn-refrain is basic to the music-piece and incorporates a touch of the "call and response". The tail end of three recurring lines is accented by *Yes, Yes!*, a "response" to the "call", *I know I got religion*. Usually the lead line is sung by a single voice but it is not rare for the whole body assembled to sing the lead line and accents of the "response" supplied by male or alto voices(lower scale).

The several stanzas here noted are secondary in prominence to the musicality of the refrain. The music of the refrain is the song. The stanzas are ornamental rather than necessary. Whereas the possibility exists that these stanzas are original to the hymn-refrain, two of them appear in other songs in slightly altered forms. There are some quatrains that "travel" from song to song in the oral tradition of Black Sacred Music.

This hymn illustrates earlier mention of the secondary concern of rhyme to meter(syllables). In performance, in this hymn as with others, the metric pace is all important.

The stanzas are interjections that underscore the basic message of the song enunciated in the hymn-refrain. The reader will note that whereas the rhyme is secondary in concern, it does appear. A slight bow is made to rhyme in the second and third stanzas and fully respected in the fourth.

Contemporary Significance

This "old time" praise song provides testimonial declaration of an essential Bible truth. "...ye must be born again." No devotee of the Christian faith can claim kinship to Christ without a crystal-clear sense of the "second-birth". The confidence of being changed (conversion) is the initial stage of Christian growth. The stanzas remind us despite being in the twentieth century, God possesses the power and option to deliver his servants from difficult circumstances in spectacular fashion. The miraculous is still in our midst. The sequence of theological truth moves immediately to reinforce the reality of struggle and suffering as a part of the Christian discipline. The last stanza evidences the continuing awareness of the rightful connection between true religion and social circumstance. The implied message of this hymn is as contemporary as today's newspaper. The message is both universal and timely.

LORD HAVE MERCY

LORD HAVE MERCY

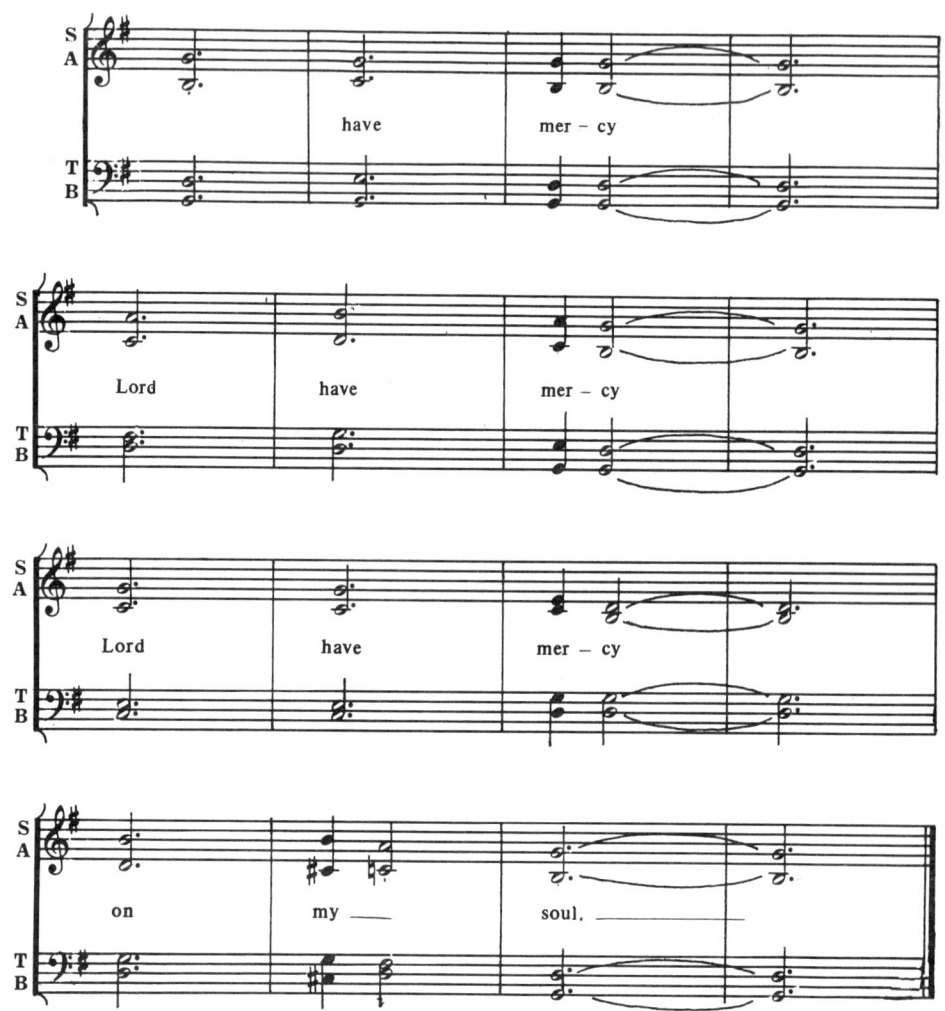

LORD HAVE MERCY

Lord have mercy,
Lord have mercy,
Lord have mercy,
On my soul.

Lord I need thee,
Lord I need thee,
Lord I need thee,
Save me Lord.

Lord please answer,
Lord please answer,
Lord please answer,
One more time.

Heal my body,
Heal my body,
Heal my body,
Make me whole.

Cleanse my spirit,
Cleanse my spirit,
Cleanse my spirit,
Cleanse my spirit,
Make me pure.

Send your power,
Send your power,
Send your power,
Right now Lord.

5

LORD HAVE MERCY

A Prayer Chant

Introduction

This prayer chant is a variant on an old theme, musically speaking. Frequently in prayer and praise services, a worshiper would express his or her deepest longings in folk poetry that is without rhyme but with specific balance suitable to the musical form chosen or created spontaneously. Some were sung, never to be heard again; others continued to live through the oral tradition common to the music of the Black religious experience. The chant form is the most adaptable because it requires only three or four syllables. Once the chant form is established by the leader, improvisation within the texture of the hymn itself, becomes quite simple and straightforward.

I first heard this prayer-chant as a child in southern Jersey among Black Christians whose cultural and religious roots were in Virginia and North Carolina. I re-discovered it after completing my studies at Colgate-Rochester in this field. Louvenia Saunders, a native of North Carolina often led this prayer-chant in our mid-week service. Sometimes the effect of this "old time" hymn would have a mesmerizing effect on those gathered in His name.

Biblical Basis

There are any number of Biblical references that mirror the sentiment of this chant. None is more appropriate than the Fifty-first Psalm:

> *Have mercy upon me O God according to thy loving kindness: according to the multitude of thy tender mercies, blot out my transgressions.*
> *Wash me thoroughly from mine iniquity and cleanse me from my sin.*
> *For I acknowledge my transgressions and my sin is ever before me.*
> *Against thee, thee only, have I sinned, and done this evil in thy sight...*
> *Behold, I was shapen in iniquity: and in sin did my mother conceive me.*
> *Purge me with hyssop, and I shall be clean: wash me and I shall be whiter than snow.*
> *Hide thy face from my sins, and blot out all my iniquities.*
> *Create in me a clean heart O God and renew a right spirit within me.*

This poignant prayer of penitence is attributed to David. Its traditional reference is to his sin against Uriah the Hittite that was exposed by Nathan the prophet.[1] It is a litany of deep remorse for the king's adulterous affair with Bathsheba. The root of this chant is that same godly sorrow for some offense against the will of God.

Theological Mooring

One enduring aspect of the folk-religion of Blacks on the North American continent is personal intimacy of a wayward child before a loving and merciful Father. The first stanza clearly states the need for pardon in the face of wrong-doing(*Lord have mercy*). In recognition of that wrong-doing for which forgiveness is being sought, the supplicant asks for God's presence in her/his life(*Lord I need thee*). The human circumstance is such that the frame of reference is not new and the evidence of previous prayers for forgiveness is registered(*One more time*). Improvement of behavior must begin on the inside and work its effect on the outside(*Cleanse my spirit*). The true believer knows that God is able to heal physical ills as well as spiritual ills (*Heal my body*). All efforts toward right living(righteousness) must have the Holy Spirit as the source of power to change life for the *better(Send your power)*.

Lyric and Form Analysis

Lord have mercy	a
Lord have mercy	a
Lord have mercy	a
On my soul	b

The literary form of this prayer-chant is probably the most common of several. The a a a b form of three identical lines and a closing second line occurs frequently (as previously noted) in this genre of Black Sacred Music. The matter of rhyme in this music is secondary to a verse-form that fits the modal form of the music. That is not to suggest that rhyme does not occur at all. Some other examples with rhyme have already been noted.

The imagery of this hymn is not of especial note. In fact, in the chant-form, very little imagery is necessary or required. The nature of the prayer-form is explicit enough without the baggage of special imagery. This prayer-chant is intensely personal and reflects musically and poetically, the quality of a lament. In performance, this hymn brings to remembrance the "Sorrow Songs" of an earlier time. Those whose musical tastes are European-oriented, will probably find this piece musically boring because of the inherent repetition of the verse and the music-form. The technical name for this characteristic is *incremental iteration*-repetition in the lyric line as well as the melodic line. This characteristic was a necessary memory aid in the pre-literate period of our ancestors and betrays its facility for the oral tradition of the Black religious experience.

Musically, the category of this hymn is a "chant", so named due to the musical form as well as the abbreviated verse. Chants of the Black religious experience are the primary illustrations of the spontaneous character of much of the music of this tradition. In the ecstasy of worship, some saint's emotion overflowed in a burst of song, cryptic but expressive of some personal experience in the Lord that must be shared. Black Pentacostalism is well known for its patented chants of "Thank you Lord" and "Yes Lord" interspersed with other short verses that fit the musical modality. As noted before, chants have not always survived the moment of their creation. A few have and this prayer-chant under consideration is one.

Contemporary Significance

The contemporary value of this prayer-chant is both cultural and religious. Our African antecedents make its survival crucial. Given the pervasive, systemic racism abroad in the land, Black people have the best opportunity to know who they are in Black Church life. If the Black Church buys into imitating white worship styles indiscriminately, it will strip itself of its cultural base. The end result is that worshippers will become *culturally*, Euro-Americans with Black faces!

Members of the oppressed community have no hope to adequately resist their oppressors without a clear and unmistakeable sense of identity. No other quarter of American life has preserved the evidence of our African roots better than the Black Church. The chief reservoir of those Africanisms that have survived, is the music of the Black religious tradition. Thus, retention of the various styles of musical traditions reinforces an accurate awareness of self. When Black people are at worship, they must employ music that is relevant to their social predicament. The existence of the Black Church is an evidence of our response to racism. Care must be taken not to jettison our primary cultural cargo- the authentic music of the Black religious experience.

I'M GLAD I GOT THAT OLD TIME RELIGION

I'M GLAD I GOT THAT OLD TIME RELIGION

I'M GLAD I GOT THAT OLD TIME RELIGION

I'm glad I got that old time religion
I'm glad I got that old time religion
I'm glad I got that old time religion
   I'm glad, I'm glad, I'm glad.

On Monday, I got that old time religion
On Monday, I got that old time religion
On Monday, I got that old time religion
   I'm glad, I'm glad, I'm glad.

On Tuesday, I got that old time religion
On Tuesday, I got that old time religion
On Tuesday, I got that old time religion
   I'm glad, I'm glad, I'm glad.

On Wednesday, I got that old time religion
On Wednesday, I got that old time religion
On Wednesday, I got that old time religion
   I'm glad, I'm glad, I'm glad.

On Thursday, I got that old time religion
On Thursday, I got that old time religion
On Thursday, I got that old time religion
   I'm glad, I'm glad, I'm glad.

On Friday, I got that old time religion
On Friday, I got that old time religion
On Friday, I got that old time religion
   I'm glad, I'm glad, I'm glad.

On Saturday, I got that old time religion
On Saturday, I got that old time religion
On Saturday, I got that old time religion
   I'm glad, I'm glad, I'm glad.

On Sunday, I got that old time religion
On Sunday, I got that old time religion
On Sunday, I got that old time religion
   I'm glad, I'm glad, I'm glad.

I'M GLAD I GOT THAT OLD TIME RELIGION

A Round-style Hymn

Introduction

With this hymn, we are introduced to a distinct form in the *Prayer and Praise Song* family. I call this type "round-style" hymn because of the unique lyric style identically similar to several others. *I'm Glad* possesses all of the identifying earmarks of the class of sacred music under consideration: *repetition, Biblicism*, the *a a a b* poetic form etc. Its uniqueness is in the *Monday, Tuesday, Wednesday*, etc. progression. Two other songs come immediately to mind in this mold: *"Something Happened When He Saved Me"* and *"I Know His Blood Can Make Me Whole"*. The former is of Alabama origin and has a slightly different lyric form whereas the latter is similar in form to "I'm Glad", with only a slight variation in the lyric form.

This hymn-type in performance allows the worshippers gathered to "participate" by standing on the "day" of their public profession in Jesus Christ as Saviour. In evangelistic or revival services, the use of such a hymn aids in identifying the "unsaved". Only those persons who have made a declaration of faith would be standing once the "round" of the hymn is completed. Those seated, presumably, are candidates for discipleship. Most importantly, it is a hymn-type that induces specific personal involvement of the individual worshipper.

Biblical Basis

Any consideration of the Biblical basis of this *Prayer and Praise* hymn is rooted in its precursor, the *Spiritual*, "Gimme That Old Time Religion". It is obvious that this music-piece is a straight-line descendant of that old spiritual. The almost identical verbiage belies its musical ancestry. The orginal spiritual makes a specific reference to the First Century Church; "It was good for Paul and Silas...."[1] The clear inference is that New Testament style faith has staying power in the face of adversity and persecution. The direct transfer of the "old time religion" idea to this prayer hymn, carries with it, implicity, that same Bible reference. It is then arguable that the rest of the "theological freight" accompanies the transfer above. The "old time religion" will make you "love everybody" and "take you home to glory". These two additional stanzas of the original spiritual have Biblical foundation. Jesus' admonition to his disciples that "...ye love one another even as I have loved you..."[2] is certainly a Biblical basis for "loving everybody". The New Testament itself is replete with the conditions pertaining to eternal life. Any reference would match the stanza, "...it will take you home to glory". This is, in a clearly secondary sense, the Biblical basis of this *Prayer and Praise* hymn which is both explicit and implicit. The "old time religion" idea is the basis for this conclusion.

Theological Mooring

The "old time religion" idea mentioned earlier is the linch-pin of this hymn's theological mooring. It seems that as we grow older, our nostalgia grows deeper. That same tendency is evident in religious reflection as well. As the sunset of life draws near, we are more aware of our mortality. We are all prone to some fantasy that in another time and another place, things were different, maybe better. There is a little of that nostalgic fantasy in this song. However, nostalgic or no, at bottom, the "old time religion" is a tried and true formula: God must be first; perserverance, faithfulness, stewardship of gifts, the inevitability of death and the assurance of eternal life. All are themes sounded in the original spiritual and the variety of forms in which it is sung. All of the ideas mentioned are both Biblically based and theologically clear. Some older forms of this spiritual include stanzas that declare "It was good for the Hebrew children"[3] and "It was good for the prophet Daniel", both of which are fixed historically during the Persian exile.[4] Again, that verbiage- "old time religion"-is presumed to be a direct transfer to this later hymn under consideration and thereby claims the same Biblical basis.

"Old time religion" works for the true believer. There is no change of life to which it does not speak and offer its succour. "Old time religion" is by it own account, Bible-based, explicitly as well as implicitly. The Bible is, if it is anything at all, the best record of God's interaction with humankind. The chronicle of that interaction embraces the evolution of the most highly developed religious discipline in history- Christianity. The moral principles and ethical demands of Jesus of Nazareth are unmatched in any of the world's religions.

Once again we are startled by the spiritual sensitivity of these rural Blackamericans who developed so deep an understanding of the dynamics of the Christian faith in their attempts to cope with the rigors of white racist America.

Lyric and Form Analysis

This hymn-type, though unique in its lyric form, falls poetically into largest group extant, three identical lines with a closing second line. It is increasingly apparent, that the *a a a b* poetic form is the most frequent in this music.

I'm glad I got that old time religion	a
I'm glad I got that old time religion	a
I'm glad I got that old time religion	a
I'm glad, I'm glad, I'm glad.	b

The origin of the Monday, Tuesday, Wednesday etc. progression is unknown to me though I would hazard the guess that it has an African connection. In 1972 during my study at the University of Ghana at Accra, I visited a congregation of the Musamo Disco Christo (Army of Church of Christ), one of the "Spiritualist" churches. These are the churches of Ghana which were organized by the indigenous people in response to the perceived paternalism of the white Protestant mission enterprise. In one of these Sunday services, a "birthday march" was held in the course of the worship service. It was a device to provide an opportunity for a special offering. With spirited music similar to the Gospel music found in Black churches in America, a line of individuals formed according to the day of the week on which they were born (every self-respecting Ghanaian *knows* the day on which he or she was born!) and subsequently danced their way to the offering table. The experience of this single instance is not conclusive though it is a clue as to where all of this might have begun. I do know that there is extant today in several regions of Africa, exact melodies that match well-known spirituals in this land. It would not take much to presume that if melodies made the journey across the Atlantic five hundred years ago, so might have the practice of "round-singing" of the days of the week.

In a recent conversation with my mentor in African studies, Kofi Asare Opoku, I asked him to read the preceding paragraph to test the validity of my *African connection* theory. He responded enthusiastically in the affirmative and pointed out that an additional clue in this regard is that in Africa the week *always begins with Monday*!

So far as the melody is concerned, it is distinct unto itself. Of the several other "round-style" hymns of this family of music, each has its own distinct melody and none are even remotely similar. The poetic form of one is *a a b a* and another is *a b c a d*, a rare form. The others follow the *a a a b* form for the most part but possess a distinct melodic line.

In performance, this is one of the most exciting of all *Prayer and Praise Hymns* because of its emotion-inducing character. The reader must keep in mind the powerful dynamics that are at work: the religious setting itself, the message of the hymn, the repetition and most important, the individual identification of nearly everyone gathered on the most important event of their lives- the "born again" experience in Jesus Christ. The physical act of standing as a witness on one's day provides the testimonial character of the hymn-type. All that has gone before congeals to produce a musical religious experience that is maximized with enthusiasm. If you doubt this assessment, the next time you're in an informal praise service, "raise" this hymn.

Contemporary Significance

It has not been said before and this is as appropriate a moment as any to mention the underlying purpose of this work. This writer earnestly believes that this family of Black Sacred Music needs to be preserved in some permanent fashion. The need is more crucial in this instance because of the oral tradition out of which this music has been born and developed. The context of the United States and the dominant society is a literary one. *That which is not written down- published- has little chance of survival.* The *Prayer and Praise Hymns* of the Black religious experience are a music art-form. What presently remains of its legacy is in the hearts and minds of the present generation of the Black aged. If this treasure is not mined and preserved *now*, we risk losing it forever!

This hymn-type is especially precious, not only because of its uniqueness of form, but also because it displays that direct transfer of the Bible-based theological understanding that has been so important to Afro-Americans in their pain-pilgrimage in North America. "Old time religion" has been the "bridge that brought us over". The use of this hymn will continually remind present and future generations of "how we got over".

I KNOW MY NAME IS WRITTEN THERE

I KNOW MY NAME IS WRITTEN THERE

I KNOW MY NAME IS WRITTEN THERE

I know,(I know), I know,(I know),
My name,(My name), is there,(is there),
I know,(I know), I know,(I know),
My name is written there.

On high,(On high), On high,(On high),
My name,(My name), is there,(is there),
On high,(On high), On high,(On high),
My name is written there.

Be sure,(Be sure), Be sure,(Be sure),
Your name,(Your name), is there,(is there),
Be sure,(Be sure), Be sure,(Be sure),
Your name is written there.

Thank God,(Thank God), Thank God,(Thank God),
Our Name,(Our Name), is there,(is there),
Thank God,(Thank God), Thank God,(Thank God),
Our name is written there.

7

I KNOW MY NAME IS WRITTEN THERE

Assurance of Life Eternal

Introduction

This hymn traces its roots to the hill country of Kentucky. Traditionally it was and still is sung at communion services. It is, so far as I know, one of a kind, though it fits the general profile of the music under consideration. Its most pronounced characteristic is the "call and response" device utilized by the lead singer to guide the assembled worshippers through the message of the hymn which is religiously challenging to all present. It is both testimonial and evangelical: it makes a statement of faith about one's personal salvation and reminds its hearers that everyone must stand in judgement.

I was introduced to this *Prayer and Praise* hymn by the Reverend Henry Jones, a native Kentuckian and presently a pastor in Cincinnati, Ohio. We shared a return flight from our national convention (PNBC) several years ago and I mentioned my great and abiding interest in this particular music-form. He quickly volunteered to teach me this hymn right there on the airplane! Jones related to me at every communion service, "old Sister Bailey" would "raise" this hymn at Pleasant Green Baptist Church where his father was pastor.

Its musical style is more akin to a prayer chant than having an identifiable melodic line. It displays a raw, primitive quality that is rare in this family of musical literature.

Biblical Basis

The Book of Revelation in the New Testament is earmarked by its eschatological symbolism. At the Judgement, disposition of one's soul turns on one's listing in the "book of life":

And I saw the dead, small and great, stand before God: and the books were opened: and another book was opened, which is the book of life: and the dead were judged out of those things which were written in the books...."[1]

Another reference is made to those who remain faithful:

He that overcometh, the same shall be clothed in white raiment: and I will not blot his name out of the book of life, but I will confess his name before my Father...."[2]

In the 20th chapter, Judgement is descriptive and final: "*And whosoever was not found written in the book of life was cast into the lake of fire.*[3] The assurance of salvation is associated with the "name" metaphor: *To him that overcometh will I give to eat of the hidden manna, and will give him a white stone, and in the stone a new name written....*[4] The "name" reference is drawn directly from these sources.

The "name" reference is not peculiar to this body of music. Protestant hymnody includes the "name" reference in several instances. *Is My Name Written There?* is a hymn greatly beloved within the Protestant family of Christians. A camp-meeting hymn proclaims:

There's a new name written down in glory:
And it's mine, O yes it's mine,
And bright angels tell the story
Of a sinner who's come home.
O there's a new name written down in glory:
And it's mine, O yes it's mine

> With my sins forgiven
> I am bound for heaven
> Nevermore to roam.⁵

In another place in this work, reference was made to the Spiritual *I told Jesus it would be all right if He changed my name*, which carries the significance of "name" to salvation.

The references above are not exhaustive, only illustrative of the phenomenon's presence among New Testament Christians, Black and white. The common source is the strong and picturesque account of John's vision on the isle of Patmos. Revelation is clear: unless one's name is written in the Lamb's book of life, no entrance can be gained to the kingdom of heaven.

Theological Mooring

The theological basis of this music-piece is hinged to salvation in Jesus Christ. The Biblical reference is explicit but the meaning is implicit. The context of Revelation and the "name" in the Lamb's book of life has to do with fundamental Christian eschatology- last things and judgment. Only those who are acceptable on the basis of New Testament requirements will be registered in the book of life. Eligibility is two-fold acceptance of the grace of God that is in the Lord Jesus Christ *and* evidence of that acceptance through obedience to the ethics and morality required of all disciples. It brings to mind the clear remonstrance of Jesus that "*...everyone who cries Lord, Lord shall not enter the kingdom of heaven...*" but exclusively those "*...that doeth the will of my Father in heaven.*"⁶

The reader is reminded of the central purpose of Revelation's writing: the early Church was being subjected to severe persecution by Roman authorities on one hand and the external and internal buffeting that accompanies the establishment of a new religion in a secular world on the other hand. John's message to the churches in Asia Minor was to keep the "faith" no matter what. The ultimate future belongs to the faithful in Jesus Christ. Thus, high premium is placed upon those whose "faithfulness" is recorded in the Lamb's book of life.

The testimony of this hymn is a faith-declaration that encompasses the confidence of the believer as well as the ultimate trust in the power of Christ (Good) over the anti-Christ (Evil) in the spiritual Armageddon that is always at hand. The believer locates the registration of "my name" as being "on high"- in heaven. The admonition is made to the company assembled that the Judgment is surely coming and every soul needs to "Be sure...etc." The final exhortation and exultation is "Thank God", the recognition that it is not by human striving that one's name is "written" but only through the love of God that is in Christ Jesus our Lord.

Lyric and Form Analysis

The uniqueness of this musical number is revealed at several points. First, its pronounced "call and response" characteristic (already noted); second, its almost slavish adherence to the rare *a b a c* poetic form; third, its lack of distinct melodic line; and fourth, the isolation of the lead singer apart from the "response" and the closing line. In the case of the latter, it is more African in musical form.

The lyrics of this hymn are very sparse, largely induced by the call and response dominance which contributes most to the extension of the lyric line altogether. Were it not for that special character, this hymn would be reduced to just a few lines. This is not to suggest that the lyrics of this music group are less than ample but only to point out the paucity of lyrics in this single instance.

Musically, this *Prayer and Praise* hymn demonstrates none of the liveliness found so frequently in this musical literature. In fact it is almost droll compared to the rest of this family of music. Its meter and timbre is more like a prayer-chant than anything else. This song is one of the few in this body of music that is measured and slow. Its form does not allow for much breadth, improvisationally. Just the opposite is true of much of the other music of this genre.

The scheme of this work has been to provide the musical notation for each *Prayer and Praise* hymn under scrutiny. The intent was to strengthen any use or performance. In this particular instance, though the musical notation is provided, my thought is that this one hymn is musically stronger if sung *a capella*. Perhaps I am persuaded to this view also because a *capella* performance would certify its authenticity.

Contemporary Significance

The central significance of this hymn in the present moment is that it needs to be preserved in much the same manner as one collects curios. This hymn is a musical curio from a specific and significant era of musical development. I have not yet been able to date these hymns precisely but I feel strongly that this is an early piece of the period under study. Its narrow musicality prevents it from being updated musically. Its singularity of form is its chief importance.

As in all of this music, the religious message is timeless. All professing Christians should have an abiding concern that their "name" is written "on high".

TALKIN' 'BOUT A GOOD TIME

TALKIN' 'BOUT A GOOD TIME

TALKIN' 'BOUT A GOOD TIME

2. When I get to Heaven, I'm gonna walk around
   Gonna ask my Lord for my starry crown

3. My starry crown gonna fit me well
   'Cause I tried it on at the gates of Hell

TALKIN' 'BOUT A GOOD TIME

Talkin' 'bout a good time!
We gonna' have a time.
Talkin' 'bout a good time!
We gonna' have a time.
Talkin' 'bout a good time!
We gonna' have a time.
Talkin' 'bout a good time!
We gonna' have a time.

I never been to heaven but I've been told,
The gates are silver and the streets are gold.
When I get to heaven (I'm) gonna' walk around,
I'll ask my Lord for my starry crown.
My starry crown's gonna' fit me well
('cause) I tried it on at the gates of hell.

I went in the valley one day to pray;
I met ole Satan on my way.
What do you reckon ole Satan say?
He said, "Young chile, you're too young to pray.
I fell on my knees and began to pray;
I made him out a liar and went on my way.

TALKIN' 'BOUT A GOOD TIME

The Blessed Assurance

Introduction

This *Prayer and Praise* hymn is pronouncedly other worldly. The Black religious tradition has historically remained under fire for being compensatory in character. This criticism is only legitimate within the context of being *overly* otherworldly or *unduly* compensatory. All religions, by nature are otherworldly and compensatory or they would not be religion. This otherworldliness is a legitimate and proper aspect of religion generally and Christianity in particular.

This hymn exhibits an appropriate characteristic of religious expression: the hope and prospect of some sort of future life that is in sharp contrast to the realities of the present life. Theologically, it is essential and desirable that the motif of the future life be sounded in balance with other verities of faith and practice. This hymn demonstrates that essential motif. It is decidedly otherworldly in its message and patently extols with great enthusiasm the prospect of changed conditions in the next world.

Biblical Basis

The theme of the after-life of personal immortality is common to all world religions. Its particularity is more pronounced in Christianity because its central personality rose from the dead. That rubric of faith is the linch-pin of the Christian believer's hope and assurance of personal immortality. Consequently, the New Testament literature is filled with references to personal immortality and the world to come that is secured by faith in the Lord Jesus Christ. Nowhere is the contrast drawn as vividly between the vagaries of this life and the joy and bliss of the next life as it is in the Book of Revelations. Revelation is, of course, a literary expression of the Christian community under siege during the worst of the Roman persecution. John the Apostle, presumed by tradition to be its author, writes in exaggerated metaphor and symbol. Much of the imagery and verbiage of the folk-religion of Blacks draws on Revelation's description of the world to come and the final Judgment. There is an overlay of folk impressions that amplify the Biblical word-pictures. The "long white robes" and "streets of gold" are surrounded by additions such as "every day will be Sunday" and greetings that are "always 'Howdy, Howdy' and never good-bye...."

In the later chapters of Revelation, the graphic description of the world to come contributes directly to the spirit and lyrics of this hymn.

Theological Mooring

The ground of Christian belief is the indisputable fact of our Lord's resurrection on the "third day morning". Paul is quite correct when he sets forth in his Hymn to Immortality that "...if Christ be not risen from the dead, then is our preaching vain and your faith vain also...But now is Christ risen from the dead and become the first-fruits of them that sleep."[1]

The family of Christian faith quite readily agrees that there is some valid question that surrounds the *modus operandi- the method* of the Resurrection, but no question about the *fact* of the Resurrection. Earnest Christians are not intimidated by the philosophical and scientific questions that the resurrection of Jesus induce. We point to the "incontrovertible evidence" that Jesus rose from the dead on that first Easter morning: (1) *The Christian Church*. The community of faith that has expanded without interruption for the last two thousand years could not possibly have survived if it were founded on speculation alone, that Jesus rose from the dead. An institution such as the Church could not exist on a rumor that He was alive *again*. (2) *The New Testament literature.* No compendium of literature has influenced Western thought and culture so much as has the rudimentary teaching of the New Testament. The germ-idea of democracy, the rights of women and children, concern for the downtrodden and oppressed-all get their marching orders from the ethics and teaching of Jesus- the central figure of New Testament writings.[2] (3) *The Christian Sabbath.* Until the stoning of Stephen, the early followers of Jesus(all Jews) observed two holy days in the course of a week; the Jewish Sabbath(Shabat) and the first day of the week to mark the Resurrection. As the centuries have rolled past, an ordinary day of the week has become a universal holy day. It is unlikely that the transformation could take place on merely the supposition that Jesus rose from the dead. (4) *The Lord's Supper* or *Holy Communion.* This celebration, universal to Christendom has its origin in the Jewish Feast of Passover.[3] Following the paschal supper, Jesus initiated this memorial event to commemorate "the death he should die...." Christians feel it unthinkable for this holiest of celebrations to have lived on the false hopes of a resurrection that never took place.

These are the four incontrovertible evidences that Christendom proffers to those who scoff at the reality of the resurrection of Jesus of Nazareth. All other Christian faith and practices are derivatives of that faith in the Risen Lord. Thus it follows that Job's heirs of trouble, the sun-kissed grandchildren of Africa, saw clearly that their ultimate hope and abode was not in this world. Amid the reality of this harsh and unbearable North American experience, they trusted in another world whose builder and maker is God.

Lyric and Form Analysis

Talkin' 'Bout A Good Time has several facets to its basic form. First and foremost, it introduces us to the quadruple *a b* form which we have not seen before in this volume.

Talkin' 'bout a good time!	a
We gonna have a time.	b
Talkin' 'bout a good time!	a
We gonna have a time.	b
Talkin' 'bout a good time!	a
We gonna have a time.	b
Talkin' 'bout a good time.	a
We gonna have a time.	b

The stanzas are a curious combination of "traveling couplets" and traditional quatrains. Most curious, is that the stanzas reflect some unevenness in an altogether different poetic form from the refrain. The first of the two stanzas clearly reflects the "couplet" form where two lines rhyme in succession. The second stanza shown is unique. Though it has the couplet form, all six lines exhibit the identical rhyme rather than changing every two lines as in the earlier stanza. The reader needs to be reminded at this juncture, that none of these hymns are "cast in stone". I have presented them in the form in which they have come to my attention. All of these hymns, however, are traditional and have undergone some slight changes because of the oral tradition by which they have remained extant.

Musically, this song is a prime example of that lively aggressive and celebrative profile of this family of musical literature. Its traditional meter or pace lends itself to lifting up fallen spirits, binding up broken hearts, holding together crushed hopes and reassuring faltering aspirations. It should be noted that the stanzas are markedly different in musical modality and match an almost uniform couplet rendition which is more of a chant than a melody. It is clipped and somewhat staccato-like in performance by a single lead singer. These stanzas are not stanzas in the strict sense of "stanza" but rather, are groupings of the traveling couplets and quatrains that suit either the fancy or the memory of the lead singer. The shift to the refrain comes only at the cue of the lead singer.

Contemporary Significance

It bears repeating that the value of these songs is twofold: first, from a religio-cultural point of view, they are an identifiable musical treasure- an art form, so to speak: secondly, the inherent theological teaching they possess makes a clear faith-statement that was necessary in the context of the sociology encountered in the collective experience of the community that gave birth to this music.

This particular hymn sounds a recurring theme common to the music of the Black religious tradition. The hope and assurance of eternal life nurtures the life spirit of the professing Christian. The pressures of the secular world around us often dulls our consciousness and sensitivity to that world of the spirit. We are prone to become so enamored of this world that we forget or push aside the reality of the world to come. Every major religion of the world embraces the hope for an after-life; Christianity has the assurance through our faith in the risen Christ and the joy of this *Prayer and Praise* hymn reflects the joy of that assurance.

POSTSCRIPT

Spirits That Dwell in Deep Woods has been a labor of love. It has been deeply rewarding to live day and night, sometimes, with these hymns of faith and trust. When sung in communal fashion, without overembellishment, they are deeply moving testimonies. Though plain and unadorned, the lyrics contain profound theological truths which our forebears captured as reflected light from the Book of books.

I indicated at the beginning of this manuscript, that this work can only be considered "seminal" in that this body of Black Sacred Music is too voluminous to be treated in a single volume. At this juncture, I have gathered more than a hundred hymn-types from all over America though all of them have pronounced "southern roots". From this collection, which is by no means exhaustive, there are twenty-four to thirty that show promise of providing significant theological thought and unique musical composition. It is this smaller group that I have chosen to focus upon. Over the period of the next two years, it is my desire to produce two additional manuscripts that will probably be titled, *Spirits That Dwell in Deep Woods II and III*.

It would be of enormous help to this writer if the reader holds in his or her memory bank any gem of faith of this genre to share at least the lyrics with me. There would be an opportunity, then, to make some analysis of its literary and musical value. Any other comment and suggestions would be welcome as well. This treasure of faith must be preserved in permanent form. God's name be praised!

Notes

Introduction

1. Wyatt Tee Walker, *Somebody's Calling My Name* (Valley Forge: Judson Press, 1979), p. 44

Chapter One

1. Old Testament between Esther and Psalms
2. Job 14:14
3. Job 15, 18 and 20
4. Job 13:15
5. Job 9:2

Chapter Two

1. Wyatt Tee Walker, *Soul of Black Worship* (New York: Martin Luther King Press, 1984), p. 50
2. II Cor. 5:17
3. John 3:1ff
4. Exodus 20:15 and Ephesians 6:5

Chapter Three

1. Matt. 11:28
2. Roman 6:6
3. Romans 12:2

Chapter Four

1. Pastor, Olivet Institutional Baptist Church, Cleveland, OH.
2. Psalm 107:2
3. John 3:7
4. Acts 16:25
5. Matt. 6:19
6. Wyatt Tee Walker, *Somebody's Calling My Name* (Valley Forge: Judson Press, 1979), p. 17

Chapter Five

1. II Sam. 12:1ff
2. W.E.B. DuBois, *The Souls of Black Folk*, (New York: Washington Square Press, 1970), p. 206

Notes (Continued)

Chapter Six

1. Acts 16:25
2. John 13:34
3. Daniel 3:1ff
4. Daniel 6:22

Chapter Seven

1. Rev. 20:12
2. Rev. 3:5
3. Rev. 20:15
4. Rev. 2:17
5. Traditional
6. Matt. 7:21

Chapter Eight

1. I Cor. 15:1ff
2. Acts 7:58
3. Luke 22:1